Pain & Purpose

"The Javar Story"

By Christina Diabate

Table of Contents

Acknowledgements

1. *Graduation Day*
2. *God Bless the Child*
3. *Daddy Issues*
4. *Everything Happens For No Reason*
5. *The Worst Is Yet To Come*
6. *Su-i-ci-dal*
7. *Living Miracle*
8. *Silver Lining "Baby Jade"*
9. *New Beginnings*
10. *Home Sweet Home*
11. *It Ain't Over Yet*
12. *Revelations*
13. *Resilience Rising*

Afterword

Resources

Acknowledgments

To My Readers,

As I pen down these words, my heart swells with gratitude for the incredible support that has surrounded the creation of this book. To you, my readers, I extend my deepest thanks in advance. Your willingness to embark on this journey with me is both an honor and a privilege.

This book has been a labor of love and resilience. In the early stages, the words on these pages felt like a puzzle I couldn't solve. I struggled to read the very sentences I was writing. Yet, it is through this process, both painful and healing, that the narrative found its voice.

I want to acknowledge the countless hours and hard work that went into bringing this story to life. From the initial spark of an idea to the final words typed, this endeavor has been a collaborative effort, and I am grateful for every hand that played a role in its creation. Special thanks to my editor, LaVonne Wallace, for encouraging me every step of the way. All the love to my sisters/ cousin tribe Baby D, Sweet "Angie" Pearl, Diana and Sharonna, etc for being there during this process. To my good, good girlfriends Lateesha Amos, Telisha Maye, Natasha Davis, Tykeiah Howell and all the countless others that encouraged me and more importantly inspired me to keep going no matter how hard it felt at times.

In the pages of this memoir, you will encounter moments of joy and laughter, mingled with tears and heartache. You will witness the tender bond between a mother and her son, forged in the crucible of adversity. You will glimpse into the depths of my soul as I grapple with questions of purpose and meaning.

But beware, for this journey is not for the faint of heart. It is a rollercoaster ride of emotions, where highs and lows blur into one another. Yet, it is within this chaos that the true beauty of our story lies.

For amidst the pain and confusion, there is a thread of hope that weaves its way through the fabric of our lives. It is the thread of resilience, of strength born from struggle, of beauty emerging from brokenness.

So, as you immerse yourself in these pages, I ask only one thing of you: to open your heart and mind to the possibility of finding purpose in the most unlikely of places. For in the end, it is not the order of events that defines our story, but the love that binds us together, transcending time and space. The story doesn't go in any specific order and the journal entries don't automatically move with the chapters to follow but it's my heart, my words and my truth.

I appreciate you all for coming along on this writing journey with me. Your excitement and support are everything. I hope the pages ahead bring comfort, make you think, and connect with our shared human experiences.

With heartfelt appreciation,

Christina Diabate

June 22, 2019

Dear Journal,

There are so many thoughts going through my head right now like…………

Are you fucking dumb bitch? You supposed to be with your fucking dying son. What the fuck is wrong with you? Why are you like this? Why would you chance not to be by his side during this time? What if he dies while you're in DC? You are a loser like Foreal. Foreal. I would never. He needs you now. Don't be a bad mother again. Don't fail him again. His father, ain't shit you ain't shit. Nah you got this. God got this. He is ok. If you don't know anything, trust yourself. And trust in God you deserve this. You worked hard for this.

Celebrate you for one moment. He ain't going nowhere because if he was he would be gone by now. Stop beating yourself up, you're doing your best. Don't be a loser again. What the fuck is wrong with you? Jade is watching. Be strong for him. You prayed about it now you have to leave it there. Like really!! What can you do? Not a damn thing, but look stupid and you're doing a good job at that already. Screaming "Why meeeeeee?" Whyyy? I played by the book. I did better than my parents ever even tried. God are you punishing me? Have I wronged you? I wasn't that bad of a kid. I just didn't know better. I know better now and I'm trying. Work with me and just keep my child for another day. Please God I need this, I need you. I need you now Lord. I need you now Lord.

Signed,

Just Keep Praying

Chapter 1: Graduation Day

I'm sitting in a football stadium-sized arena, my palms moist from me holding my phone so tight, my knees shaking, my feet persistently tapping against the hardwood floors, sweat dripping from the side of my head, like hot and cold enveloping my body at the same damn time. I was having an out-of-body experience all at once. And all I could think about was my son. Man, it is supposed to be the happiest day of my life. The day I walk across the stage to accept my Bachelor's degree. Sadly, all I could think about was Javar, my big boy, fighting for his life in a hospital bed with wires hanging all over his body plugged up to all of those machines helpless without me.

Two days had passed since he'd gotten shot, and here I was, in the heart of Washington, D.C., at the Capital One Arena a couple of hundred miles away from him. I felt so many different emotions all at once. I was furious, and so fucking angry at the cowards who did this to my son. Angry at the world for always letting me down. Most of all, I was angry at myself for being here, instead of by Javar's bedside when I knew that he needed me.

    I just sat there in that colossal stadium, surrounded by thousands of people, yet I'd never felt more alone. Tears welled up in my eyes as I tried to process it all. I felt like a zombie, so empty and lifeless, and questioning why I am even here? I had set the bar high for myself, proudly striving for a goal that no one in my family had ever achieved. But now, I was second-guessing everything and wondering if it was all worth it.

What kind of mother was I to leave my child in the ICU, struggling to survive, while she was celebrating her college graduation? *My son is lying there alone*, was the thought that replayed in my mind like a bad song. My brain couldn't even grasp what he went through that day, being left bleeding on the ground, crying out to someone for help. According to the ER physicians, "the bullet went straight through his neck, tore into his spinal cord, split his tongue in half, and knocked out his middle tooth". Who would commit such a ruthless and cruel act? Why would they leave my first born to suffer? My child is fighting for his life and continuously screaming in agony! . Those bastards left my baby for dead!!!!!!!

As I replayed Javar's cries in my mind, the usher was calling the next row to the stage. I'm trying to snap out of it, trying to embrace the achievement I'd worked so hard for. All those long nights of studying and endless papers. My family is so close but it seems like they're sitting far away and they look like tiny dots in the crowd. At this point, distance doesn't matter. Physically, I'm at graduation to receive my bachelors degree in Washington, DC but mentally, I'm in New Jersey with my bed ritten, devastated, and nearly lifeless son.

Was this real, or was it just an extended nightmare? Either way, I wanted to wake up from it, and fast. Throughout the ceremony, my hand stayed in my pocket clutching my phone, awaiting that dreading call from the hospital. I couldn't bear to think about what that call might mean—for me, for Javar, for all of us.

Some may wonder why I bothered at all to walk that stage. Why I decided to go through with it. Yes, I put in the work, but more importantly, I walked for my kids. As a first-generation college graduate, I wanted them to witness how you can overcome the toughest obstacles. I want them to understand that no matter your age or what life throws at you, you can always start fresh, finish what you started, or forge a whole new path. I had gotten the phrase 'Delayed but not Denied' written on my graduation cap—those words etched from the depths of my heart. Why, because despite all the hardships, loneliness, the feeling of being lost, and the trauma I faced prior to this moment, this experience was my personal triumph.

So, why did I feel this gnawing guilt?

I already knew the answer to that. In all reality, the only place I should have been was by Javar's bedside.

The usher was calling for the next row to move forward. At this point, I am very close to the front stage and ready to walk across the aisle to accept my degree. I was an almost 40-year-old honor student with a 3.2 GPA. What should have felt amazing has my stomach in knots. I look into the crowd to find my family, but no one is in the spot they once were. What the fuck? Did they really leave as I am about to walk across the stage? Neither them nor my baby boy will be there to see me walk. It was so disappointing and the day was really becoming worse by the minute. I look to the left and my family isn't there. I look to the right and I can't find them anywhere. I am literally in the line to walk across the stage and there are tears in my eyes again. I just want to see baby Jade's face. I just want him to know that I'm doing this for him. I can't procrastinate any longer, so I take a few steps until I reach the top of the steps, my head hanging low with sadness and disappointment.

As soon as the Dean of Students announces my name, a group of my friends and my family arrive through the big crowd, screaming, "We love you Tina!" above all other noises. To my right, in the corner, there is a big sign that had 'Delayed, not Denied' written on it. My Tribe carried that sign as they scream and yell my name to make sure that I know they are there for me, as well as being strong and proud of my accomplishments.

Jade appears on the side of the upper seats right above my head and screams, "Mommy, you are my hero!" He almost jumps out of the section and into the crowd, right into my arms. My heart is pounding and the tears are flowing, knowing that everyone is making a way to show up for me, even when I am giving up on myself. That was nothing but God. God always sends you these priceless moments that help heal your heart. And in that moment of clarity, for just that one second, the audience was calm, silent and my heart was at peace. The love was vibrating at a high frequency and it was just what I needed to press forward.

After my graduation ceremony, despite being surrounded by love and support, I couldn't shake the sadness of not being by my child's bedside. Nevertheless, being the first college graduate in my family is a significant accomplishment, and I hope it sets a powerful example for my child and future generations. GENERATIONAL CURSES When they say, 'It runs in the family", you tell them, 'This is where it runs out'!

"Strength in the face of heartache: Holding on despite the pain tearing at my soul."

Chapter 2: God Bless the Child

Before I delve deeper, let's start from the very beginning. I was born into hardship, and just like most people from my neighborhood, we were welfare kids. There were three of us, all girls, with me being the oldest. My mother and father were both addicted to drugs, even still to this day. At fifteen years old, my high ass mother gave me permission to live with my oldest son's father and his family. I was only fifteen years old. It's so crazy when I think about it now. What sane person lets a fifteen-year old baby girl go live with her boyfriend's family?

My story is one that has been told by many little, lost black girls growing up with a mother and father who lost themselves. When you have to fend for yourself, you learn the hard way that you have to work for anything that you want. In those years, I shoplifted for my sisters and myself to survive. I stole new clothes from Macy's, and the local mall, so that they didn't have to go to school looking like I did and get picked on for not looking 'fresh' or stylish. My father wasn't far, but he was around. One of the key factors contributing to my father's absence was his battle with addiction.

Addiction affects not only the individual, but also their loved ones. Substance abuse simply consumed him and led him down a path of self-destruction and isolation. My father's addiction to drugs became his primary focus, and overshadowed any responsibilities or commitments he had towards his damn kids. He was in and out of jail most of the time and as my mother struggled with her own addiction, as well. Most of the time, the whole situation just left us confused. Some days she would be in the attic smoking weed with us and the next day she would be chastising us. I'm sure it was a battle that wasn't easy for her to fight, especially with defiant teenagers like us. I feel like my parents did the best for us with the best that they knew. They couldn't do for us what wasn't done for them. We really were badass little kids. We were definitely out of control because we had been on our own for so long and we didn't honor authority from anyone, not even the police. There was one person that I looked up to, my Aunt Sissy, who I'd always admired and adored. Even though she was a recovering addict, she still was able to take care of her home and she always made us feel safe while at her home.

We usually had dinner at her house every night, with family time, just watching TV and enjoying each other's company. We couldn't do that at my house and with my mom. She always had a new man and that's where all of her attention went. She didn't have a job, so she did whatever she had to do to feed her drug habit. In that room, behind that locked door, for hours a day, there were all kinds of foreign noises coming from that room. As kids, we wondered what was happening up in there.

The worst part was that she didn't even do it to help us. All those men in there, all those times, were just to feed her drug addiction. I always wondered where she met the men that didn't do drugs but would allow her to do them. They had to be some losers to fuck with a crack-head. Not just fuck with her, but some of them even loved her. I can only imagine how low their self-esteem was. I'm sure they were and are possibly still dealing with some of that trauma.

I remember one night, I was like 10 years old, and she was drunk. Her boyfriend, at the time, came into my room trying to 'feel me up'. I was on the top bunk bed and I felt him, even in my sleep. I woke up kicking and fighting. It didn't take much to fight off a drunk, overweight, middle-aged man. He didn't want to wake up the rest of the house, so he left me alone. The entire time this was happening, my little sisters were on the bottom bunk sound asleep. I never really mentioned it to anyone afterwards and I didn't think much of it until I realized one day that he was trying to molest me. To this day, that fucks me up to even think about it.

That wasn't the first time I was around men who were pedophiles, especially in my family. As an adult, I reflected back to my uncle, my mother's brother, always recording us girls with his camera, while we were dancing and shaking our behinds. That was some real weird shit. This man loved us to entertain him, and he would put our heads under the covers and tell us to bend over and dance while he recorded behind us. We were very young and didn't think anything of it. But, as an adult… what the fuck kind of weird, freaky, shit is that? Later on we found out that he was the same uncle that molested our mother and as she now admits, ran her straight into her drug addiction to escape the shame and guilt. The fact that her family chose not to 'tell on' the other family member either? That's truly a difficult situation to endure.

To think about it, even my little sister was molested. My father threw the guy who did it out of an apartment window, in Pioneer Holmes. But, that wasn't really any justice because the same guy had probably touched a lot of other kids after her. So, why wasn't he arrested? It just goes to show you how chaotic this world is that we live in. So many other deeply rooted dysfunctional black families that live by the same notion 'what goes on in this house, stays in this house.' What kind of crazy mentality is that to have and pass onto your children?

Some days, my mother would feed us bullshit, like ramen noodles with ketchup while she took her good food into her bedroom, such as fried chicken and chocolate cake. Did she not think that we wanted to eat fried chicken and chocolate cake, too? It was small things like that I'd remember about my childhood. The things that stood out to me. The same things that I would never do to my kids. The generational trauma that was more than likely done to her as a kid as well. Let's be clear I am not saying that she wasn't a loving mother doing her best. She was just as ill prepared as the mothers in her family that came before her.

In middle school, I would steal jeans from the laundromat on Madison Ave.. I had every color of Levi's jeans. I feel so horrible thinking back on it. I would rob people after school just so I could get something to eat at McDonalds and not have to come home to some bs food she set aside for us. It would mainly be helpless, white girls, but I was no thug. I thought I was merely doing what I had to do to survive. We had a clique called The Stick-Up Girls, which consisted of me and a few of my friends who also had parents addicted to drugs or similar circumstances. We would hang around the school and prey on so-called easy targets and rob them for their coats and jewelry. We were so dumb and bound to get caught sooner or later. One time, I got caught and almost went to jail as an adult. Karma showed up for me when I was twenty-three years old. A kid that I'd robbed and injured badly, took me to court for restitution. I was only fifteen years old at the time of the incident, facing charges at 23 years old, scared to death of paying the price for something that I did when I was a very young, and a very different person. Now when I think about that black, shearling coat and the name chain that I'd ripped off that Spanish girl's neck, I know that it was not worth it in the first place.

My whole world changed when I turned twelve and I met my first boyfriend and soon to be baby father. I used to babysit for my cousin, who later died in a tragic, drunk driving accident. She'd worked the night shift and needed me to watch her kids overnight. What kind of parent thinks it is a good idea to leave their teen daughter alone at night, free to do whatever she wants? Mine. So, my young teenage-love, boyfriend, aka baby daddy, and I played video games during the times that I babysat, if you know what I mean (hint, hint)! We were both so bad at it. I scratched his back up pretty badly the first time we had sex. I'd seen it in a porn movie and thought that's what you were supposed to do. I'm almost 100 percent sure that to this day, he still has those marks on his back. He was fifteen years old and I was twelve years old. I was searching for the love I didn't receive at home and the attention and affection that he gave me was the closest thing to that. Just like I said, I was truly a lost, little black girl.

Around that time, my mother acted like she had lost the fight with us all and had given up on raising us. Her solution was to allow me to live with my baby daddy's family at the young age of fifteen. It's not a lie. I was only fifteen years old. I truly believed that his mother and family loved me dearly because when she noticed me sneaking over to the house and hiding in the room, she just told me to stay and live there. Now, thinking back, I realize how it was such a shitty move for both sides, but it was something that made me so happy at the time. I finally had a safe place, a home, a family setting that wasn't controlled by drugs.

Of course, this didn't last long because his grandmother really just wanted someone to help her clean her house from top to bottom. I was literally a modern-day house slave. That creepy house had everything covered in plastic, from the rugs to the floors because she was a neat freak, and borderline OCD. She could tell right away if anything in the house was out of place. She had hoarded so much stuff in that small house, that it was nauseating, even though it was neatly organized. The last straw was when I came home one day to my baby daddy having sex with his ex-girlfriend.

I left and went back to my mother's house and it was even worse than when I'd first left.

Now, it was like a raging crack-house. My baby sister, Baby D (the name speaks for itself), and my cousin 'ran' the attic, which meant that all of their drug dealer friends were selling to our family, who were getting high with their friends on the first floor. It was a revolving door of 24-hour action in that house by the bridge on Jefferson Avenue. This nightmare didn't last long though because one of the crack-heads fell asleep, while smoking crack and burned the place down. But this was the reality of my life, so when it should have broken me down, it didn't because I was so used to the dysfunction that I just adjusted.

I've come to a profound understanding of just how challenging my upbringing was. I had my first apartment in my grandmother's basement at sixteen years old and at seventeen, I was emancipated and given full-custody of my two younger sisters. My mother and father had signed the paperwork before I'd even arrived and left the courthouse before I could get there. They didn't even fight me on anything. They literally signed over all parental rights for their young children to a seventeen-year-old kid. I guess they figured I could do a better job than what they were doing.

To an outsider, I was another statistic. Doomed to be a teenage mom. Boy did I ever live up to that stereotype! I ended up getting pregnant and had Javar at the young, tender age of eighteen. I remember one day, walking outside, looking very pregnant, and an older woman from my old neighborhood looked at me, and said, "Finally." At first, I looked at her with confusion, then disgust, just thinking about how quickly she'd passed judgment on me instead of uplifting and giving me hope in a seemingly hopeless situation. At that moment, I grasped the severity of my predicament. I was surrounded by crack-heads and people who had lost hope for themselves, not people who encouraged me to become a successful adult. I was just a baby raising a baby, and a high school drop-out. And just like most young mothers, my child was forced to grow up with me.

At my big age now, and as a parent of two very highly energetic boys, there's no way in the world I would ever entertain some of the things that I was allowed to do as a teenager. But sanity is not a trait of a drug addict because their attention span is only geared towards that next high. Worrying about what a child does or doesn't do is not important. In retrospect, I can see that my life was very similar to a roller coaster ride and I basically learned how to ride the waves, the highs and lows.

When I think back on it, I realize that I had a very troubled upbringing. Sometimes, I sit and wonder about what I ever did to have had this type of life. Dealing with my childhood. Dealing with all of the pain and suffering I've experienced with my own child, Javar. I tried my best to always do the right thing and I was there for him in every way possible. I provided for him and made sure he was better than good, although he would probably say the opposite and that I was too strict and I didn't let him do anything. Honestly, that was just my way of trying to protect him from this cold, cold world. Well, we all know how that turned out. No one can ever say that I didn't try. At least I tried.

May 20, 2017

Dear Journal,

It's 2 am and we're all asleep in bed and I get a call from Javar that he had been in a car accident. A what??????????????? mofo, a goddamn car accident. This stupid dumbass fucking kid of mine has fucking really lost his fuckin mind. I mean like this time "sighs", like wtf. I know you fucking lying, runs to the window…. Guess whose car is missing my mofo Benz truck. "Screaming"Blackkkkkkk gtfup I need to go fuck Javar high yellow ass up. He stole my car and crashed it. Let's go now. We wake baby Jade up and get him into the car. We ran out of the house barely dressed. On the way there all I could think about was how I wanted to protect him and beat his ass at the same time. I wanted to act like I was the driver when the accident occurred. If we get there in enough time I'll jump in the driver seat and say it was my fault at least he won't get in trouble or it won't affect his license. My dumbass, thinking way too far ahead. Get to the scene................. it's a 3 car pile up. This goofy mofo flipped the benz truck side swiped 2 brand new cars. We pull up and he is sitting in the back of the police car. I run up to his ass and just start swinging on him like wtf is wrong with you. Do you know what you did? He was crying, Ma I'm so sorry, I didn't mean it. Check out the backstory: this lil goofy mofo has been stealing my car and joy riding when I take my sleeping pills at night and knock out. This night he just happens to wanna get on snapchat and floss. He literally was on snap chat when the accident occurred. Tell me that's not the goofiest ish you ever heard. I gotta get some rest now. This shit done worked my nerves. I just can't even deal. I will deal with his ass tomorrow.

Signed,

I don't want to go to jail tonight!

Chapter 3: Daddy Issues

After years of not talking to Javar's father, I mean absolutely no contact at all, my sister gave me his number and I tried to reach out to him about Javar's behavior. I wanted to tell him that we needed to do an intervention for Javar because I knew he was headed in the wrong direction. He had been following a bad crowd or either trying to be "down" and I knew that it would lead to a long road to nowhere. Nothing good ever came from the streets. I knew that, and his father knew that, so I thought that by having him speak to him, father to son, it would all make sense and be better received by Javar. Boy was I wrong!

His father immediately got angry with me and told me that Javar was a man now and that he had to deal with the consequences that came with life. I quickly hung up the phone on him. Then I remembered why I didn't have any contact with him in years. He was never emotionally or mentally mature enough to deal with anything serious and I knew that he was still dealing with his own demons after trying to commit suicide due to his wife and twin babies dying during childbirth. This guy has been bat shit crazy all his damn life. Oh, how quickly I forgot the time that this maniac came to my job and smeared shit all over my car and his **child's car** set after finding out that I wasn't going to be with him any longer. Don't even ask why, because he had got married and didn't tell me and I was supposed to still be with him no matter what. The audacity! After being together for more than ten years off and on. Boy did, the tables turn and when they did. He aint like the way it felt. On this day, he literally caught the 24 bus to my job at UHaul on Frelinghuysen ave and smeared shit all over the interior of my car. My poor little hooptie would never be the same. My boss at the time came to the back of the store with a awkward smirk on his face, He said ya crazy baby daddy fuckin ya car up. Jokingly, We already knew that he was up to no good. I just ran out the store chasing him down the street with a hammer. He ran for his life for a few blocks. He for sure knew that if I would have caught his ass I would have beat him real good. After dealing with so many unorthodox situations like this with this unrealistic person I now had to call my baby daddy. I knew that this wasn't someone that I could reason with. Even about his own flesh and blood, his first-born son.

We would all feel the wrath of his father's words soon enough.

In some ways his father was right, even though his delivery wasn't good. Javar was an adult and he would soon see the consequences of his behavior. The sad part is, we all felt the consequences because in our family, when one cries, we all cry. And we have been crying for two years. But it seems like we will be crying for a lifetime.

After things fell through with Javar's father, I tried to reach his grandmother who had been my support system since birth and especially since Javar's father was completely absent. And to clarify, if being absent meant literally living in the next city over in Newark NJ, living his own life and having several more kids, then yeah, that kind of absence. Grandma Pat was a blessing and a curse. From the day Javar came home from the hospital, she was there and she taught me everything about being a good mom. She bathed him every day. Yes, I said every day. She came to my house everyday for the first two years of Javar's life. Back then I would say she was too intrusive, but now I can truly see she was a blessing. We were young parents and we had no clue how to raise a child. She wasn't going to let us fuck it up, not with her first grandbaby.

She spoiled him rotten! And she was everything that my mother wasn't for him and me, and even so much more. We have had our ups and downs. Shit, we even came close to throwing blows in the past. Still, she couldn't see Javar doing no wrong, no matter what.

Even after we saw the trouble coming and he changed from that innocent, sweet boy who spoke proper English (no one understood how when his mama was so ghetto, correction: loud, outspoken, and rough around the edges, while he was so well spoken). It was easy really. I had chosen to take Javar out the hood at an early age. No more ducking bullets in my old neighborhood on Catherine Street. No, I didn't want any of that for him. So, we kept moving further south, away from Elizabeth. Most people would say living in Linden wasn't that far-fetched from living in Elizabeth, but to me, the cops were always present and a lot of the activities from my old 'hood' didn't take place in my new neighborhood. Of course, bad things happened everywhere, but not as often in Linden as opposed to Elizabeth.

Grandma Pat lived in Rahway, not too far from where we lived. At this point, I don't know if she was following us or we were following her. But we were never too far apart. Like I said earlier, she played a major role in my son's life even though his father was absent. She was a big and bold presence. She is a good woman, No, a great woman! She was hardworking and didn't take shit from anyone. She was a real 'Newark Girl'. She'd had a bout with cancer and was living life on her own terms now. For the most part, that meant traveling more and just trying to enjoy her life, which was something that had only been a fond memory because working twelve to fourteen hour days before she'd been diagnosed with cancer was the only life she knew. Now that life had literally made her sit down, she could finally stop and smell the roses. Well, at least she could smell the dirty, Bayway River.

Yo, lemme tell you 'bout the day Javar's piece of shit ass father showed up at the hospital while Javar was laid up in the ICU. Dude had been a ghost for months, then suddenly he wanna roll up and start talking' crazy to me. I was fed up with his BS, man. Couldn't take no more from nobody, ya feel me? So, he picked the wrong day to fuck around and find out.

Big Goofy starts yelling', tryna blame me for Javar's situation, sayin' I ain't been a good mom to our kid. Straight up callin' me all sorts of names, calling me dumb and all the things he was deflecting away from himself. But I'm like, "hold up", I've been holdin' it down for 19 years, taking care of our child all alone. So, who does he think he is talking to?

Now, let me backtrack to a funny story when this country dog(baby daddy) shows up at my apartment, acting' all entitled 'cause he found out I got his lawsuit money from child support. Man, it was a cold December day, and he showed up wearing a cheap blazer and a tacky knock off Gucci scarf straight from downtown Newark. He's begging' for a cut of the money, talkin' 'bout he needs some J's or whatever. I'm like, nah, bruh. You've been MIA for over a decade, owing me thousands in back child support. You really think I'ma give you a dime?

So, he starts talking' crazy, threatening to knock over my brand new flat screen TV right by the front door where he was still standing looking slow. But I ain't sweatin' it. I'm just chillin' with my newborn baby, Jade, laughing at his sorry ass. When he peeped when my sister Baby D and my husband Black were home, he suddenly had a change of heart and bounced real quick, with no fuss. In the end, he dips out quietly, realizing' he ain't getting' nothing' from me and takes that walk of shame to the 24 bus stop. We all burst out laughing.

    I look back at these moments and just shake my head. I never had an active father and neither did Javar. I guess we both had "daddy issues." However, despite all the drama, I went above and beyond for my son, standing strong against the nonsense. It's a reminder of the strength and resilience I have always had, even when clowns try to bring me down.

January 10, 2019

Dear Journal,

You can really be everything in this world for your kids and you still won't get it right. You can spoil them and give them the world and still not get it right. You can provide them with all the opportunities that were never given to you because you lacked what you lacked you poured into your child ten times over and you still might not get it right. I pray day and night about this child. I pray he gets it right. I pray that he sees that I just want the best for him and all that I never had. I pray that he gets it and doesn't see me as the enemy but as his momma, the woman that will be by his side through it all when everyone is gone, when all the fake love disappears, when the tears dry up and there is nothing to smile about. I hope he knows that I pray for a shield of protection over his life every time that he leaves my door. I pray that one day he doesn't break my heart and if he does I will find the strength to heal from it. This is my prayer for my son.

Signed,

Keep praying for change.

Chapter 4: Everything Happens For No Reason

The morning of the shooting was like something out of a nightmare. It felt as though time had slowed down, yet everything was moving at the speed of light. It was as if I was caught in the middle of a whirlwind, watching chaos unfold all around me. Tears streamed down my face, mixed with disbelief and intense pain. On that fateful morning, Kia, a close family friend, pounded on our door urgently and the look on her face sent shivers down my spine.

I had spent the previous night at my sister's house, blissfully unaware of the tragic news that was about to shatter our lives. We had stayed up late, laughing and enjoying each other's company, completely oblivious to the darkness that would take over our lives.

When we finally let Kia inside, she collapsed to the floor, her screams piercing the air. "Javar is shot! Javar is shot!" she cried out, her voice trembling so much she could barely get the words out. Those words echoed in my mind, as I refused to let them sink in. I desperately wanted to believe it was some sick joke, a cruel prank, a poorly thought out trick. But the fear on Kia's face told a different story. She pleaded with me, "Please, Tina, we have to go now! We have to get to the hospital!" At that moment, I knew. I knew that this nightmare was all too real, and I had to snap out of it. Without a second thought, we raced to the hospital, the journey feeling like it took an eternity. As we arrived, a bunch of familiar faces greeted me, their expressions full of sadness. I could sense the gravity of the situation before anyone even said a word to me, before the doctors shared any information about Javar. The nurses guided me to his room, and what I saw will forever be imprinted in my memory.

My son lay in the hospital bed, his face unrecognizable. Besides the swollen eyes, Javar's mouth was so bloody and swollen…his mouth, my son's mouth, was evidence of the bullet that had entered through the back of his neck and exited through his mouth. His front tooth shot out and his tongue split in half by a bullet! My son's precious face was now an unrecognizable sight as a result of a senseless shooting. No parent should ever have to witness. Yes, you read it correctly the first time. Let's pause, go back and reread that sentence. My own flesh and blood, the child I had nurtured and watched grow, had been shot in the most unimaginable way. My son was shot for no reason. The reality of it all is still too much to bear.

From that day forward, I was a shattered woman. The pain from watching my child suffer was unbearable and I felt helpless. I longed to take away his agony, to shield him from the cruelty of the world. But in that moment, I realized that some things are beyond our control. This was a reality I never thought I would face, a nightmare that became all too real.

That day marked a turning point in my life, a moment when I had to confront how fragile life really is and the randomness of it all. Javar being shot shattered my perception of the world and left me questioning everything. But even in the midst of the darkness, I still believed that everything happens for a reason, even if that reason is not yet clear.

Dear Journal,

God I know you hear me it's me again begging for forgiveness for myself for my child help us Lord. I can't take it any more… The nights are longer than the days… the worry doesn't stop. I'm weak. I need you now Lord..or just take me. Do you even hear me? Are you there? You said you would never forsake me or leave me alone… I'm alone again. I really can't do this shit any more… I'm fucked up and I just don't wanna be here. This life ain't fair. Nobody gives a fuck about me. I don't even care about me. I'm a shell, a mere existence of life. What kind of life is this to suffer for so long? I don't belong here. This is not my path. Why do you hate me so much? Is it all the bad shit I did? I'm so sorry. Please forgive me. Help my child. I can't see him like this. This is hurting me more than him. How can I go on this way? I'm tired, I'm weak. I'm weary. I have nothing to give.

Signed,

Keep fighting!

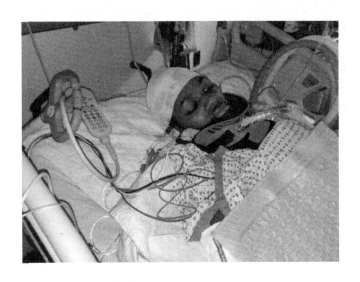

Javar's incredible resilience: Despite soaring temperatures and medical challenges, he kept pushing through. Even with his temperature hitting 106°F and six weeks of cold blanket treatment, he never gave up.

Chapter 5: The Worst Is Yet To Come

As I laid on the floor of the ER, tears burned my face, the doctor's words echoed in my head. "Paralyzed from the neck down." Those words hit me like a ton of bricks, shattering the life I once knew. How could this happen to my son? How could he end up like this? The guilt I had was overwhelming. As his mother, I was supposed to protect him from harm, but now he was lying in a hospital bed, fighting for his life. The days that followed were a blur of doctors, nurses, and machines beeping in the background. I was in a constant state of shock, trying to come to terms with what had happened. But no matter how hard I tried, the reality of the situation was too much to bear.

My son was never going to walk again. It was like a punch to the gut. All the dreams and aspirations I had for my son were gone in an instant. He would never be able to play sports or run around with his friends like he used to. He was confined to a hospital bed, hooked up to a ventilator for the rest of his life. My heart ached for him.

As the days turned into weeks, I watched my son fight for his life. He was a fighter, that was for sure, but the road ahead was long and uncertain. We had no idea what the future held, but one thing was for sure, I was determined to be there for him every step of the way. To be his rock when he was feeling weak and to make sure that he never lost hope.

And that's exactly what I did. I spent every waking moment by his side, doing everything in my power to make him feel loved and supported. I knew that the journey ahead was going to be tough, but I was ready to take it on. For my son, I would do anything.

September 11, 2019

Dear Journal,

I'm really fucking losing it. My paranoia is at an all time high, I'm scared of my own shadow, my nerves are so bad. I feel like someone may be watching me. I don't sleep now. I'm looking up at my window to see if someone is going to come through and kill me. I will never live on the first floor again. This is dum just go to sleep. Nobody doesn't watch ya goofy ass (me to myself). Every night after spending my entire day in the hospital with Javar I come home in the early morning hours after drinking as much as my body could handle. To enter my building complex I have to walk down this creepy path that is poorly lit and long as fuck or atleast it seemed in my mind. My crazy ass always had to have some kind of weapon in my hand. Walking with the keys between my fingers like I'm gonna key someone to death. My mind is playing tricks on me. I hear things in the bushes, my heart beating fast as hell, palms sweaty, just walking fast and making it home only thing running through my head. I see objects in my rear view mirror. You know what the mirror says: objects may be closer than they appear. Yes, I know and by the time they creep up on me. I'm going be already gone, because I'm going to pass out from delirium. Someone is fucking watching me or is my mind playing tricks on me. Am I hallucinating from lack of sleep? Come on God give me a break this is too much. You must want me to hang it up. How could anyone handle all of this? How could anyone just keep going when everything is telling them to just give up, I can't do this shit! I'm really losing my fucking mind. Send help or something bad might just really happen.

Signed,

My mind is playing tricks on me.

Chapter 6: Su-i-ci-dal

For weeks, correction, for months following the senseless shooting of my son, I was literally a walking zombie. Each day, I had the same routine. Shower. Get dressed. Go up to the hospital to be by my child's bedside. That's what a supportive parent does, right? We get up, handle our responsibilities and not show weakness. Imagine, watching your child suffer ev-er-y day! Now imagine still having a younger son at home to raise while barely making it through the day with his hospitalized brother.

Now my nights went a little different. My nights consisted of alcohol and drugs. No, not the kind my parents used but I got pissy drunk and took sleeping pills. This was in hopes that I never wake up again in this horror story that I didn't want to star in. That's really how I felt. Honestly, I didn't want to wake up in this situation another day. Obviously, it didn't work.

It was easy for me to numb myself because during the day, I just kept going and going. Sometimes, I'd give a smile to someone here or there, but my life had become a mundane routine. I drove to the hospital without even noticing where I was going. I parked my car in the visitor's lot and didn't remember how I got inside. I brought the same foods everyday. I saw the same faces along my route. My eyes were glazed and most people who knew me and looked at me, could see right through my soul and know that I was not me. I was physically there, but I'd mentally checked out.

Why did this happen to me? What did I do to ever deserve this life? So many emotions swirled inside of me. Hurt, guilt, shame, and disbelief submerged every inch of my body. I proudly wore it like a badge of honor. Anyone could see the pain in my eyes. You could feel it when you hugged me. I was inconsolable.

I was broken into a million pieces. In my head it was all my fault. I felt like I should have done better for my child. All he wanted to do was smoke weed in my house and I ran him away. Were my realistic expectations for him not realistic? Was I so hard on him because my past experiences could easily become his future? What I would do to turn back the hands of time! I would definitely do things differently if I had known this would be the outcome. Nothing made sense. Not the shooting and definitely not my life.

Some nights I would go to the crime scene, sit and drink myself into oblivion. I would sit in my little car and chain smoke Black & Milds, staring at everyone, wishing a mother-fucker would. I was clearly out of my mind. One night I even provoked a few situations. I saw a few young people hanging out looking like they were up to no good. I approached them, asking for weed. I know I looked dumb as fuck but I did it anyway. They were like, "Get the fuck out of here, lady."

I said, "Fuck all y'all! Lil' bum ass niggas, y'all not gettin' money out here, anyway! Lil' dirtbag-ass lil' niggas not gone do shit to nobody! I will light this whole fuckin' block up! I wish you m'fuckas would say something dumb to me!" They could see I was drunk, they talked a little bit of shit but they weren't really stunting me.

Honestly, I don't know what I wanted out of that situation at that time. I didn't have a gun or a weapon of any kind on me, either. I had asked everyone I knew and even offered to buy a gun. No one would sell me a gun or even point me in the right direction of where to get one. Now that I look back, did I need one? Was I provoking those boys so I can harm them, or did I unconsciously want them to harm me. I'm at the crime scene of my son, drunk, with no protection. Obviously, I wanted trouble and hoped they'd finish the job unlike the Lil' Niggas that tried to kill me son! Another failed attempt.

I had one more great idea. I'll just put out a hit on the suspect that shot Javar. This was before I decided to let go and let God. I made a public post on social media asking for the person that robbed my son to be "unalived" for $10,000. Yes, "unalived" because I didn't want to be reported for making death threats on social media. This wasn't even a desperate cry. This was just a lost soul looking to hurt someone else just like I was hurt. The crazy part is, I had some people saying they would do it for me. I even came very close to exchanging hands with the person that I knew for sure was a hitter and would get the job done. But something just wouldn't let me do it. As much hurt I felt, my family felt, I couldn't do that same thing to them or their families.

    The crazy part of this whole situation is that the hired hit man that was going to complete the job for me ended up getting killed just a few years later and his family is living with the pain of his death, to this day. I couldn't continue on with the hurt and pain. I had to lay down this burden and I had to give it all to God. It was too heavy to carry.

In the midst of the chaos, God spoke to me and said, "Revenge is mine child, you don't have to worry". My family and friends saw my pain and hurt but knew that wasn't who I was. I'm sure that more than likely, they thought that I was more suicidal than homicidal. However, that plan didn't work out either. I was literally out of my mind, a ticking time bomb. I was gone, and in one of my last attempts to get revenge, before God finally sat me down. I let Him take it from there.

Dear Journal,

God, I come before you as I am willing to give you my heart. Take it and do what you want with it lord. I have felt that pain that should have taken my life but yet I'm still here. What is the purpose of this pain? What is the purpose in this pain? I'm hurt, I'm lost. I'm scared and I can't do this alone, Lord. I don't want to. I give myself to you. God, I am in my own way if I stay like this I will die. I don't want to die, in fact I want to live in spite of all my pain. In spite of all the hurt that I feel and will probably feel for the rest of my life. I wanna live, and this is not living. Staying in this hurt is not helping me. I have to give it to you, God. It's heavy and the weight is too much to bear. I want my heart to be light again. I wanna smile again and not be angry and sad all the time.

I cannot change the things that have happened. GOD please heal me. Make me stronger because this battle isn't over and I need you to build me up so that I can live to fight another day. Please God.

Signed,

Keep fighting for another day.

Chapter 7: Living Miracle

Javar was a miracle by many standards because he wasn't expected to live through this; he wasn't expected to make it this far. But not without complications. He had been in ICU for over four months and then transferred to rehab where he'd resided for three more months. Yet again, Javar's body was fighting against his mind to stay alive.

I remember when I sat in the ER, and watched the doctors and nurses pump on my son's chest, with millions of wires and tubes connected to his body, everyone running around frantically trying to bring him back, how I sat in a chair, in the far corner of the room, as everything was happening around me.

I was numb and lifeless once again since Javar's shooting, which had happened months ago.

My ongoing battle. From months of no health issues at all to issues occurring daily, I had simply become numb. No tears would fall from my eyes because they were all dried up. This was a horror scene playing over and over in my head, daily.

I didn't know if I was not there mentally or just absent from my body. I didn't feel anything at all or because I didn't know if he was going to live or die. I just didn't feel at all. I was there, like many times before, because I was supposed to be there. This was just another recurring nightmare that I had to complete an episode of. I'm sure the nurses and doctors wanted to tell me to leave the room and they may have even done so. I wouldn't have heard them even if they did. I was just there, sitting with a blank stare into an empty world that had taken all my hope away. I was at that same dark place, once again.

Chapter 8: Silver Lining "Baby Jade"

Flash back 10 years before this incident, I had been married to my then husband "Black" and we had just given birth to a beautiful, vibrant little boy and named him Jade. Jade saved my life way back then and I didn't even know it. He gave me a reason to want to live again after being depressed and downtrodden for so long. Jade's conception was not a mistake, but I never had any plans on having more children even though I was married. In fact, I was that friend who advocated for abortion because I didn't ever want any more kids. I don't know if it was because I'd had such a hard time being a single mother with Javar, because my pregnancy was so terrifying or if I didn't want to bring more children into this cruel and wicked world. Honestly, after Javar's birth when I busted the blood vessels in my eyes during labor in pain and agony, I never wanted more kids. I understand that I can be overly dramatic, but any woman who can endure the intense pains of labor, despite its beautiful outcomes, deserves lifelong honor as a Goddess. It's as if we're tearing our bodies apart, feeling as if we're crushing 100 bones simultaneously.

    Around the time that Jade was born, I was working at Blue Cross Blue Shield of New Jersey (BCBSNJ) as a phone rep and I hated my job. I cried every day because I was an emotional mess and I was never properly taught how to manage and deal with my feelings. Growing up, I was always very emotional being a thug Pisces and all. A tough cry baby.

I don't know what made me say one day, "GOD, I hope I'm not pregnant," but I said it and then I was pregnant six weeks later. Honestly, I thought about getting an abortion, but I just couldn't go through with it. I don't know why I couldn't do it. It's not like I haven't had an abortion before. Like I said– I'm anti-kids. But, for some reason, this particular time, I just could not complete the task. I had even attempted several times. I realized Jade was sent to help me heal. There's no way for me to know if my story would have been different or if I would've come out of the mental fog after Javar's incident, if Jade hadn't come into my life. Back then, I was so busy dealing with Javar's health issues, that I had been apart from Jade for close to six months. To protect his innocence, we didn't let him know what had happened to his brother. Then, one day he told me that he already knew.

When Javar came home from the hospital, he and Jade developed the best relationship. Although Javar was now disabled, he was still a very bright boy, and sometimes he would help his little brother with homework and play phone games with him using his assistive technology. In addition to that, he would provide direction to Jade with household chores or doing things around the house. At that time, they were so close that Javar's room was the only room that Jade would sleep in and you'd find him sleeping most nights on Javar's futon.

Most days, you would catch them in the room talking for hours. Then, things slowly began to change. A few months after he came home, Javar became so angry towards everyone and Jade avoided him most of the time. After that, the only time he spent with Javar was just to check on him and see if he needed anything. Then, he would leave right back out of the room. This was the case for everyone taking care of Javar had become so hard. He became so mean and I didn't know if it was because he resented that he was paralyzed, lying in the bed on a ventilator and everyone was living their life, but Jade and I were right there with him everyday at his beck-and-call. We didn't deserve to be treated badly by him. They say the caregivers get treated the worst and I can testify to that. I ended up joining caregiver groups and found a new therapist that just dealt with a caregiver's grief. One more "head doctor" to add to my growing list. Just what I needed.

Dear Journal,

Today was a good day. Jade and I did early morning yoga and we went to church. This church family is so welcoming. I felt at home as soon as I got there. We have been visiting for weeks now and I'm ready to make a commitment to this church, New Beginning Ministry. The name says it all. It's a new beginning for me and my life nothing is the same. But for God, while beginning my journey to find the purpose in this pain I was placed here for healing and nurturing. Pastor Tami and sister Hafizah are such a breath of fresh air they have even came to the hospital to pray with Javar a few times, Jade enjoys childrens church and he had a great performance with the praise team one Sunday. I'm going to do it next week. I'm going to commit to this church and give my life to the lord once again. This church was conveniently located in Elizabeth, NJ they rented the funeral home as a temporary space. How ironic I was having praise and worship in the same building that I would soon have my son's home-going service in. We know the building is merely a shell and the spirit is what came into the service every week that we attended church there. But it was very ironic when I think of people, places, and things that God placed in my life during this time.

Signed,

Keep Praying. Keep Fighting. Keep Living.

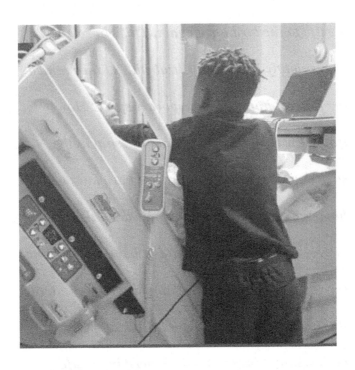

Jade's first time seeing Javar in his condition, he automatically went into help mode and wanted to do anything to help out.

Chapter 9: New Beginnings

Finally, we made it home. Javar's health was constantly improving and my family thought it was the right time to surprise me with my baby, by bringing Jade to me at the rehab center. It was a surprise indeed! He saw me and ran to me, like he never wanted to let go. His hug surrounded my soul with joy. The joy that I once had before all this happened, the joy that I needed to keep pushing forward. When Jade looked up at me and said, "Mommy, I don't want to ever leave you again," the rest was history.

Jade is my dance partner, my food critic, and he helps me cook and clean around the house. He reminds me so much of Javar when he was younger and sometimes, I'm just a little bit scared that one day the outside world will be a bigger influence to him than I am.

Before the lockdown during the pandemic; I didn't have time to focus on anything at all, only what was going on with Javar. We were restricted in-person visits and could only talk on the phone or visit him at the window. So often, I remember telling Javar that he was an adult and even though he was in this situation, he was still able to do so many things with his life. Javar was equipped with the best assistive technology. With a tap from his cheek he was able to control his phone, tv, and the lights in any room he was connected to. Even though he was paralyzed from the neck down, Javar was very active on social media. He also had an unlimited amount of resources at his disposal.

Javar was in a transitional state in his life and the outcome of this situation was completely dependent upon him. How he chose to look at life, even in his situation, was crucial because he was an adult and needed to be his own advocate. Now, was the perfect opportunity for him to be the adult that he could be and this time no one was there to hold his hand and speak up for him. He had to open up his mouth and be the strong young man that we always knew he could be no matter the circumstances.

Even Though the Covid-19 lockdown kept me from visiting Javar, it was a blessing in disguise. No, that's not true. The true blessing was that I didn't have to run back and forth to the facility all day, every day, but I still worried about him a lot. I mostly worried about the hospital staff taking care of him properly, if he was eating well, and his overall mental health. He was so stubborn throughout this whole process that I think I'd only seen him cry once. But, I knew that mentally, he had to be distraught. If I was going insane in my mind, what was he going through? He showed little to no emotion at all. He was just there in shock and disbelief of his new state. I always wondered how he could be so tough and strong.

For the first few months I went to the bathroom so he wouldn't see my face or ran out of the room just to cry alone. This was an ongoing thing and he showed no emotions at all, just disbelief and great disappointment. The disappointment came from the friends that stopped visiting after the first week. Shit, the first day. All of the friends that he desired so much to be like were nowhere to be found. Long gone, and living their lives as if nothing had changed at all. Maybe a, "Damn that's messed up," phone call once in a while, but nothing more. That was something that I had to get used to myself. I wanted everyone to be so supportive, but in reality, life does go on and people do have their own lives to live. That was one of the hardest lessons that I had to learn, yet one of the realest that I hold near and dear to me, to this day.

During the pandemic, I learned to be silent. I learned to be calm and be okay with not being okay. There was a stillness around me and a sense of peace. Something that hadn't been there in a long time. A peace that only God can give you. I focused more into studying, meditating and personal healing. I did yoga and studied daily affirmations, constantly praying and worrying less. It was a surreal feeling, but I felt relief, as well. I found a church home that welcomed me with warm arms. It's as if they knew that I need to be loved very badly. The first time that I went to service, I was greeted and treated like a family member. I knew this would be my new church home. Every week I could feel the spirit coming over me and I felt like a new person more and more. I was gaining understanding of the unknown and I was learning to be okay with that. The bible says, "You can't pray and worry, so don't worry about tomorrow, because tomorrow will have its own worries. If you worry about tomorrow you can't enjoy today" (Matthew 6:34).

December 2, 2020

Dear Journal,

There was a breakthrough in the clouds, a moment of clarity when the storm seemed to be over and we were coasting towards the new normal. In preparing for Javar to come home I knew that even though we had overcome some of the toughest days of our lives it was sure to be more to come. We were all so happy to get Javar home and try to create a normal life for him and ourselves. I wanted to create an environment of healing and hope. I created giant size motivational mantras to go on the wall of my room and Javars room. Although at times I know that Javar didn't want to see it. But it was a constant reminder of how far we have come. It read, "Be Thankful for what you are now, and keep fighting for what you want to be tomorrow". This would leave an impact on anyone that entered into Javars room when they visited him. They would always compliment on the living space and tell me over and over again that I'm doing such a good job. In my bedroom my motivational Mantra which I still read every morning to this day says. "Everywhere I go I prosper. Everything I do works out for me". I am attracting unconditional love, abundance, clarity, high vibrational experiences, and sacred connections. I am thriving in every way. Things are becoming more clear for me. I can celebrate my life.

Signed,

I got this!

Chapter 10: Home Sweet Home

Eventually, we arrived home after enduring persistent struggles with Javar's health. Deep in my heart, I strongly believed that my son would benefit greatly from being in a loving and supportive family environment, receiving the care he needed. After over nine months of being in several different facilities from his injuries, Javar had finally come home. He was in better shape than we or the doctors had ever expected. This child was told that he wouldn't make it past a few days, but he had beat the odds. Day by day, he was striving for better, and I knew it was time to take my baby home. With all the support and help that I was receiving from the nurses and therapists, I knew that I could make my son feel even more comfortable in his home and hopefully surrounded by more family.

The process to get a grown man-child, who was paralyzed from the neck down, from living in a long-term facility to live at home was nothing short of trivia. It took us weeks of setting up life-sustaining equipment, ventilators, a wound care bed, tray table, etc. I had to basically set my house up like a hospital. His grandmother and I went all out for him! We made sure that our child came home to the best care possible.

To help encourage his mindstate, I had a mural painted on the wall that stated words of affirmation. We hung a TV on the wall and created a great living space and even better space for healing.

The day Javar came home my stomach was in knots. I literally shitted like ten times that day in anticipation for his arrival. The way he was transported home in an ambulance, with a respiratory nurse and a driver, was a full on show and I'm sure he wasn't too happy to be paraded around like he was hurt. But he really was happy to finally be home.

After Javar had been home for a few days, the calls and visits stopped, so it was just Jade, Javar, the nurses giving around-the-clock care, and myself. What we thought would be such a smooth transition would turn out to be just the beginning of a lot of hard work. I could see the pain in my child's eyes as he watched the world go on around him, the friends that he wanted so much to be around only visit once in a while. He was capable of making calls, but most of the time, even when he made calls, his friends and family were so busy living their lives, they barely answered. Each day, he was getting angrier and angrier and the only people around to take his anger out on were us.

    I tried my best to make his life as pleasant as possible in his situation, but it didn't change the fact that he could only move his head and no other part of his body. He regretted being alive and if I was being honest, I did too. I had imagined a much better life for him, one that was full of all the things he desired. Just living his life, free to explore the world and finish college, ready to start a career or even take over one of my businesses. He never had any interest in doing that but it was a dream of mine. He was so smart but he seemed to give up. Some days, he wouldn't wake up to eat breakfast and he didn't want any light coming in from the windows, in his room at all. This was a sign of depression that I had known very well.

I did everything to bring him out of the darkness, but anyone that suffered from depression would know that the only thing to bring him out of the darkness would be Javar. Every morning I read the mantra that I'd placed on his wall. "Be thankful for what you are now and keep fighting for what you want to be tomorrow," because in my head I was going to do whatever it took to restore whatever life that was possible for my son.

But he was addicted to his phone and looking at people on social media. It was his only source to the outside world while he recovered from his injuries.

I'm sure that played a major, mental fuck on him because he knew that he was lying in that bed, unable to move his body. If he was anything like me, I knew he could name a few people in his life that had done things that made them deserve to be like he was or even worse for it, but he had gotten the short-end of the stick and was bound to misery. Reduced to watching everyone else go on and live their best lives, or so it seemed. The thing about social media is that people only post the good things, to make you believe that life is good, while on the inside, they are probably hurting, as well.

We all have our own battles to fight, even if we think those battles are bigger than the ones we face. I went into debt purchasing the best handicap accessible vehicle to transport my child, to be able to take Javar to his doctor's appointments, to dinner, hell we even had high hopes of a family vacation, like a road trip. It was my job to try and do my best to give my boy back some of his life, and I was going to do it by any means necessary. We visited a restaurant for the first time in over two years as a family. We were accompanied by Javar's nurse who'd cared for him over a twelve hour span of each day. I treated everyone to dinner, even Grandma Pat, and in that moment for just a second, we were a normal family again, doing the things we love together.

On another note the one thing that I couldn't get over was Javar's anger for anyone in the house. I had begun to get back to being myself before all this happened, with the nurses helping out and Javar being stable. I was trying to get some of my life back, once in a while. I would go out and to events with my friends or take a short vacation. Mama needed a break too! But I could only see the resentment on Javar's face as he realized that I got to live a normal life sometimes and he was still not able to. I wish that I was able to explain it better to him, how everything that he'd felt in his body, it was almost like I'd felt it, as well. Neglecting my self-care would ultimately lead to my demise in the long term which would lead to me not being able to care for him as well. Instead of trying to have those hard conversations, I just went on and did what I could with what I had.

I can say now, in hindsight, I wished that I would have had these conversations with him. I wish that I'd known how to talk to him like a person instead of like my child. I wish that I'd treated him more like a person before the incident and definitely afterwards. But you don't know what you don't know. And there were no adults in my family who had ever respected me enough to ask me how I felt, what I wanted, or ever respected my wishes. Now I can see why when I was able to get away from some of my family, I did. I took on the responsibilities of being an adult without ever being given the correct advice on what that actually looks like.

So even though I knew I wanted to be better than my parents, I didn't know how and in the end, I pushed my son away by not being more understandable and not reasoning with his logic of the things going on in his life in this day and time. What I would do to have that conversation with him now! What I learned in this process of the journey was that you can't expect people to be how we want them to be, when everyone is dealing with their own demons, trauma, hurt and pain. People deal with things differently. Some people run from the hurt and pain and go into silence, not knowing what to say. Not knowing how to comfort someone hurting so badly. I've seen that happen to the people I expected to show up for me and my son in our time of need. I saw it in my son when he probably needed me most, not just to care for him, but also to understand him and meet him where he was, not where I wanted him to be.

Javar finally made it home right before Christmas 2020, all of our hearts were full of emotions from the hard road traveled so far and the realization of the long road of recovery ahead. Nonetheless, we cherished every moment spent with him as a family. We welcomed New Year 2021 together. It was the greatest feeling ever!

Dear Journal,

Laying in bed singing in my head. "Lord if you don't do it, It just won't be done. Do it for me!" I'm having yet another sleepless night, tossing and turning. I can hear the machines beeping even though Javar is not here. I just can't get those sounds out of my head. Beep Beep Beep. I feel like I'm losing my mind. The conversation plays over and over in my head. Javar told me not to bring him back next time. He said DNR- do not resuscitate me. He said I'm tired, as the tears rolled down my eyes. He spoke with a sternness that I felt when he said I'm Tired. He said He thinks that he only came back last time to tell me that he had to tell me that he was at peace with everything and that he was ready to rest now. I said No, that's dumb we have come so far. I began to try and explain all the research that I have been doing about stem cell research and the chances of him walking again. He just cut me off and said no Ma. This is it. He looked tired too. After the conversation he closed his eyes and rested for the rest of the visit. Lord, I know you are sick of my shit. I'm hot and cold and up and down. But God, I don't know what to do with this. How do I process my child saying let him die? Am I selfish? Tell me what do I do? I have come this far, God don't let me fold now.

Singed,

Staying faithful and hopeful.

Chapter 11: It Ain't Over

I affectionately remember the night Javar was ailing and in so much pain. The nurse had just left my home for the night and everyone went to bed. I'd had a drink and a sleeping pill because I was tired mentally and physically drained from everything that was going on with Javar's health, and life in general. By this time, I was addicted to sleeping pills because it was the only way that I could sleep at night. Jerome, my current boyfriend, woke me up frantically saying, "Javar wants you." I'm barely awake, like every other night, when the machines start to beep, which could have been for several reasons. Javar wasn't getting enough oxygen, or the vent fell off, or a wire was hooked improperly. I ran into the room and checked all the wires. Everything was fine, no beeping noise. But

Javar didn't look too well. He said, "Something is wrong, something ain't right."

I told him, "Alright, I'll lie down on the futon and if it continues, we'll call the ambulance." I was so exhausted and depleted from all my energy from the day. Javar's facial expression changed to alarmed, "No, don't call the ambulance," he says in a faint voice. He did not want to go back to the hospital.

"I have to, because I don't know what's wrong with you," He responded.

"No! They will keep me for a long time and I won't be able to come home…"

He went on like this for a few minutes. Explaining why he did not want to go back to the hospital. I felt his pain. We had been through this cycle time and time again and he was right. But was it the right choice at this time? This is a question that honestly haunts me to this day. Would my son be alive if I wasn't too tired to force the issue and had just taken him to the hospital to get him checked out?

I called his grandmother who was skeptical just like him about going into the hospital and getting bed sores or MRSA, a deadly bacterial infection that you can get from being hospitalized, which is what happened other times that he had been admitted for long periods of time. We both laid back down and decided that if he still had problems in the morning we would go. He agreed but I can only imagine the pain that he must have been in while those things were happening to his body. Although he was paralyzed from the neck down and on a ventilator, he always knew when something was wrong. This time was nothing different. We were hesitant to go back to the hospital for all the wrong reasons when we should have called an ambulance. However, we didn't and went back to sleep.

At six o'clock in the morning, I woke up to check on my son and his stomach was swollen like a pregnant woman who was nine months along. His nurse arrived at seven in the morning and told us to call the ambulance immediately because there could be an eruption in his bowl. We wondered what was causing this and then he began to profusely throw up a black liquid. Like nonstop. As soon as the ambulance arrived, he lost consciousness. Now everyone is frantic! What had I done? What is happening now? Why didn't we go to the hospital last night? This new nightmare would be unexpected if we hadn't already experienced a lifetime of nightmares in the past few months.

When the ambulance arrived at the hospital, the doctors rushed to Javar. No one understood how his vitals were normal, but he was unresponsive. The doctors told me he was dead. He was having seizures and his body was in sepsis. They removed gallons of black fluid from his body. His bowels had backed up into his body and were attacking his organs. I'd fucked up. If only I wasn't so tired, so dumb, so stupid!. If only I'd known better, I could have done better, no matter what he said or I'd thought.

Will I ever be able to forgive myself? Will I ever be able to get over this? I couldn't forgive myself for days after Javar was back in the hospital.

I prayed to God once again why am I going through so much? What good could this mean for my life? God, as he always is such a good guy sitting up high and looking low, sent me gentle reminders all the time, in awkward ways to let me know that this fight wasn't mine and that I wasn't alone.

Chapter 12: Revelations

In my healing process I became very heavy into yoga. I would go once a day, it would be me and three or four older white women, stretching for my life. It really made me feel good. It energized me and helped relieve a lot of tension and built up stress from my body that I had endured in the past few years. I love yoga and I highly recommend everyone give it a try. And not just once. It's a different kind of healing energy and it was just what I needed to keep going on.

On this particular day, there was just myself, a much older lady and one other tall, white lady. She sat very close to me in class in a big, empty room. It felt awkward. She quickly engaged in a conversation with me and told me that her son had overdosed while he'd been away at school, at

Rutgers University. She was so warm and welcoming. She made me feel extremely comfortable and she was easy to talk to. So, I did.

I told her my story and what I was going through. Throughout that yoga session we laughed and cried together. She was a kind voice that I really needed to hear at that time. She made me feel special and filled me with words of encouragement. I was so happy to have a new yoga friend. I went back the next day looking for my friend as she told me that she would be back the next day. I was excited and ready to tell her about the day that I had with Javar after I left yoga, but to no avail, she wasn't there. I waited around after the session was over and asked the yoga instructors if they remembered the lady that was sitting next to me in yoga class. I couldn't even remember her name. They seemed baffled because my class was usually small, it was during the pandemic, and many people still weren't coming to class. Everyone knew I was the black girl with the big butt who stuck out like a thumb and no one remembered her at all. It was like she never even existed. I knew I wasn't tripping. I went to look at the sign-in sheet and it was just my name and an older lady who had attended that session. I was in such shock that I left the yoga studio. Looking up into the bright sun shining on my face, I smiled in disbelief of God's great work again.

I went on to continue my day and for days after it just felt like I had a glow about me, a little feel of lightness about my steps as I had to continue on in this journey called life or the life that had become my new normal. I frequently consulted my close friend Natasha, a nurse, about the challenges arising with Javar, such as when he needed a colostomy bag. She consistently offered me valuable guidance, emphasizing the importance of adjusting to my new reality and reducing unnecessary stress. "You've made it this far," she'd reassure me. "Just continue putting in the effort and maintaining faith for brighter days ahead."

Javar had been through yet another very traumatic experience as he was back in the hospital after his body had shut down and he was gone and in an induced coma for quite a few days. I just did what I was supposed to do. The doctors said he was gone. I'm sure that if he hadn't woken up and shown any new signs of life they may have been having a different conversation with me about after life plans. I didn't think that I had seen that baby come back to life so many times that wasn't in my thoughts. I just came and did what I was supposed to. I played his music everyday and put his phone in front of him and scrolled through social media laughing at videos as if he was laughing right along with me.

Guess what? Eventually my baby woke up. The Miracle Child was back again like nothing happened and back to talking junk to everyone. Looking back, I now realize how super strong he really was. The first thing he asked me was, "Why are you on my phone?" Unbelievable that the child was in an absent coma for days and that's the first thing he says. That was Javar with that one-of-a-kind personality unlike anyone else. He also stated that he didn't remember anything and I told him that it was a good thing he didn't because it wasn't nice to see them pump buckets and buckets of black fluid (sepsis) from his chest via a tube in your throat. I had sat there watching him convulse for days, with a faint heartbeat off and on, and was told over and over that there was no hope. But GOD!

Chapter 13: Resilience Rising

It had been almost two years since Javar survived a fatal gunshot that left him paralyzed from the neck down and ventilator dependent for life with a long road to recovery. Despite the odds, he had made an excellent recovery and was living the best he could in this new state of being, or so it seemed.

However, on that dreadful day, December 3, 2021, Javar passed away suddenly, leaving his loved ones and community in shock. I can remember the day like it was yesterday. The day before, after almost a year of reluctantly not wanting to take the Covid shot, a nurse convinced Javar that it would be great for him to take it, because of his respiratory issues. Javar had already possibly contracted Covid three times by God's grace only tested positive, but had no symptoms, which could have been because he was already ventilator dependent and wasn't relying on himself to breathe.

Javar told me the day before he died that he had decided to take the shot. I was like, "Why! You clearly don't need it."

He said, "I'm gonna take it Ma." Please remember, I am his mother and by all accounts he was a grown, twenty-one year old man and he could make his own decisions. Throughout this process, I had taught him to be his own advocate, to be responsible for making sure that he had a voice and was treated right by hospital staff when we were not present. Honestly, even if we were there, what he said was what it was. We had our usual visit and sat watching TV together. I washed his hair and braided it. After a while, we closed out our visit as per usual with I love you, see you tomorrow try, sleep well and if you're struggling, don't stay up all night, ask the nurses for sleep meds because you deserve a good night's rest we all do. I always reiterated to him that your body needs to heal, be positive, try and think good thoughts and stay in a good headspace. We can get back to where we were and build again when we get you home. Let's just work on it.

Honestly, I was not thinking of bringing Javar back home. So many nurses told me that I was so brave and strong, but in his condition he needed full care, just in case of emergencies, just like the last time. They were right and I was only thinking about what was best. I knew that having him home made him feel better. It even made me feel better. But I couldn't take not being able to help him again. I wasn't a nurse and even though I had learned so much in that short amount of time, it was still so much that I couldn't possibly know. My ride home was so long that night and it seemed like my heart was just not settled. I almost felt like something bad was going to happen, so I pulled over in my car and prayed. So many times, I had let the tension build up in my body, let it overcome me, so I was trying to learn how to release this energy and just be ok with not being ok. Not worry, not cry, not stress, but just be. Even if it was just for the night, and I could wake up tomorrow to do it all over again.

    The next day, I was so tired. Tired in my body. Tired in my mind. I called Javar and told him I wouldn't be coming to the hospital and that I would ask his Grandma Pat to come see him. She was always late, so I knew it was plenty of time for me to give her notice to feed him and just sit with him for a little while.

As the day went on, I just took time out to lie around calm and peaceful throughout the day. There were no issues and the day just flowed until around three o'clock in the afternoon when my sister called me frantically, shouting, "Something is wrong with Javar! They have been calling you and you aren't answering!"

"OK, calm down. I'm sure he is fine. I'll call now." I hung up the phone with her and called the center. They told me that Javar was having problems breathing and that they were sending him out to the hospital. I was so shocked and said, "What? OK. Just keep me updated and let me know what hospital he is going to." Then his grandma called and we talked about what was going on. We both agreed that it wasn't an emergency and that we would go on about the day until they told us what hospital he was going to. Then, we would meet up there (remember we had been through this a million times before, with Javar being rushed to the hospital due to his injuries). It was not even an hour later when I got the call that they had tried to resuscitate for more than 50 minutes and that he was no longer with us.

Confused and lost, I instantly thought, *No, this can't be happening. You just said he was fine and that he was going to the hospital. What the fuck happened?! Y'all said he was fine.*
Later, they told me that shortly after Javar was resuscitated the first time, he went into shock again

and they lost him that time. By now it's around five-thirty in the afternoon and my bright, sunny, December day had turned into a gloomy dark one. The transition was surreal. One moment, I was sitting in full daylight and the next my house was covered in complete darkness. I screamed so loud that it alerted Jade, and he ran into my room and said, "Mom, what's wrong?"

I said, "Javar is dead."

His screams echoed mine, but even louder. He just kept screaming and crying out, "I want my brother! Take me to Javar, Ma, take me to Javar! Let's go now!" All I could do was sit in the dark, in shock, in the middle of my bed. No facial expression, no emotion, just complete shock. Numb once again. As the family began to come over to console me, I saw the love that Javar had from so many people and I decided now was the time to celebrate his life. I didn't want to be sad in front of these people. I decided that I had to show my strength and hold it all together. Hold it all in.

For days, no tears would come out of my eyes. My face was expressionless now I had been hit with the task of burying my son. Everyone kept asking me, How can I help? It was such an ignorant question. Can you bring my son back? Can you heal my heart? Can you take me away from this life that has been nothing but pain and suffering seemingly my entire life? Can you unalive me right now?

The day before the funeral, my family and I had to go and see his body. I was sick to my stomach. I didn't want to do it. I couldn't do it. Why did I have to do this? What kind of sick shit is this? Why is this happening to me again? A new fucking nightmare to keep me up all night because I had to see my son lying in a casket? That's not the way that it's supposed to be! He is supposed to be burying me, not the other way around! I broke down in my car, crying and screaming, but I still went to the funeral home. I waited outside for my family support team and sister/cuz crew. When we walked into the funeral home doors, the anxiety immediately left my body.

There was a smile on his face, when I walked closer to his body. A smile that said, *Mama, I'm OK and I'm free now. I'm with God now you don't have to worry anymore. The dream is over and you can rest now. Lay your burdens down and give them to God. It's too heavy to carry and I'm assuring you that I'm OK in this new realm of spiritual life. I have made it to the King! My legs work and I'm walking around streets paved of gold. I'm sitting on the right side of the Father and now I'm watching over you.* The tension left my shoulders, a weight was lifted and I felt good that my baby was at peace.

The day of the funeral or The Show, which is what I call it. The Big Show is a funeral for the people that weren't there and now get to be there to see him one last time. I hated the whole idea. I didn't want anyone to see my son dead. In fact I didn't want to see him dead either and I wanted him to have a closed casket service. All I could think about was, why the fuck do these people get the honor to see my son once again? Why? He was here on this earth for two years after his incident, so where were you then? Why didn't you care enough to come sit with him and share some encouraging words then? You weren't there! No, it was me there, every time. All the hospital emergency visits, that led to days and sometimes weeks, it was me there with him. I was there when he was in a coma for days, non-responsive, no sign of life in his body. You don't get that pleasure. Fuck you! Fuck all of you! This is not a show. My son is not on display for viewing like he;s in a museum. I was so full of anger and rage I didn't know what to do with it.

I have suffered severe depression and anxiety off and on, especially during holidays and his birthday because I miss him so much. I can go on and live my life knowing that God has guided my child into the best home ever. I chose to unlock my heart and to forgive myself and all the burdens that I had gone through. After my heart had been broken by God, by what I thought was Him letting me down and not healing my son. In fact, how could he even let something like this happen to us in the first place? I was leaving it all behind and I needed this healing and forgiveness for myself. I needed to forgive the people who did this to my son. I needed to forgive my mother and father for not being the ideal parents that I wished I had. I needed to forgive, open up and let my restoration bring back my hope. All of the anger that I was carrying weighed heavy on my heart and if I'd let it consume me, it would eventually kill me.

So, moving forward, I choose life and love and laughter, this day and forever. And now when people see me, they say, "How do you do it? No one would even know that you have been through what you have been through." And I would tell them, "I gave up that anger, hurt, guilt, shame, and disbelief because what happened to me, happened to me and it almost killed me. But I choose happiness, and I choose love. I choose peace and I choose to honor my son in the best way I know how. All I can do is smile and move on. More bad days will come but it is how I respond to them that defines me. If you think about it or ever take a moment to look around the room, we are all fighting our own demons. We all think that what we are going through is so big until you hear the next person's story and then your heart melts and you want to know how they are making it through.

You make a conscious choice each day. You can be bitter, sad, or in a constant state of fear of what can happen next because of past trauma and negative experiences that you've had in life or you can highlight the good experiences, live in those moments and make them grand and bigger than the bad days. Yes, the bad days are sure to come, but it's up to us to be overzealous in those moments.

Live in the good times. Live in the moment. Dance in the rain and shine in the sun. Dance like nobody's watching, and enjoy every good moment. Continue to work towards the goals that you want to achieve in life. Surround yourself with amazing people that will lift you up and make you want to be a better version of yourself.

"Javar's favorite saying which you can see written on his graduation cap on the back cover is " Always strive and Prosper ", a meaning that lives in my heart eternally.""Always strive and prosper" is a powerful mantra, a testament to the relentless pursuit of progress and growth. It encapsulates the essence of resilience and determination, urging us to continuously move forward despite challenges or setbacks. Let it be our guiding light, illuminating the path to success and fulfillment in every endeavor we undertake.

Afterword

For too long, I walked through life with a storm of pain raging inside me. It consumed me, turned my days into endless nights, and my nights into haunting nightmares. It was a pain that wrapped itself around my heart and squeezed, leaving me gasping for breath, drowning in sorrow. I didn't understand why this had happened, and not knowing was like a knife in my chest, twisting deeper with each passing day.

But life, it has a funny way of teaching us the hardest lessons when we least expect it. I thought I'd never find my way out of the darkness, that my suffering would be an eternal prison. That's when I learned that pain, deep and gut-wrenching as it may be, is not the end of the story—it's just a chapter, a part of the process.

I remember the day when the truth finally came crashing down on me like a ton of bricks. It was like a revelation, a moment of clarity in the midst of the chaos. The moment I realized that the pain was there to teach me something, to push me to grow, to change, to evolve.

See, pain isn't just some random, cruel twist of fate. It's a teacher, a relentless one at that. It forces you to confront the darkest corners of your soul, to dig deep into your own humanity. It's like a mirror that shows you who you truly are, who you can become if you let it shape you.

I had to learn not to marry that pain, not to let it define me, not to let it be the only story I told. Pain is just a part of the process, a stepping stone on the path to purpose. It's the fire that forges us into something stronger, something greater.

They say "beauty for ashes," and that's exactly what I found. When you get tired of being stuck in the cycle of sadness, loneliness, hurt, and anger, that's when you start to see the bigger picture. That's when you realize that the pain, as brutal as it may be, is a catalyst for change.

Hurt, it can heal, but only if you let it. If you keep it locked inside, if you nurture it like a poisonous weed, it'll eat you alive, body and soul. Stay mean, stay sad, stay hurt, and that pain will break you, my friend. But when you finally decide to let it go, to release it into the universe, that's when you start to heal.

I won't pretend it's easy; it ain't. It's a journey, a rocky one. But as I stand here today, I can tell you that I found my purpose in the midst of that pain. It became my fuel, my driving force, my reason to keep going.

So, remember this: Pain may knock you down, may tear you apart, but it can also be the thing that lifts you up, that helps you rebuild. Pain and purpose, they go hand in hand. It's up to you to choose how you want that story to unfold.

In loving memory of "Javar Yurahn Carson", my dear son, great friend, cousin, and the best brother ever.

"Gone but never forgotten"
Beneath the quiet of the night's embrace,
My dear Javar took his heavenly space.
A soul so bright, my heart's sweet song,
In every memory, his love lives strong.

From my arms, he ventured far and wide,
Yet in my heart, forever he'll abide.
Through life's journey, his spirit remains,
In the gentle rustle of memories' refrains.

With each sunrise, and as the twilight falls,
Javar's laughter within my heart enthralls.
Though tears may fall, and sorrow may be near,
His presence in my soul, forever clear.

As the pages of time softly unfold,
In the story of life, his chapters told.
In the book of love, where bonds are spun,

Javar's chapter reads: "Gone, but not undone."

So, let these words be a mother's embrace,
In loving memory of Javar, a sacred space.
As life's story continues, each new dawn,
My son lives on in my heart, forever drawn.
                              -Mommy

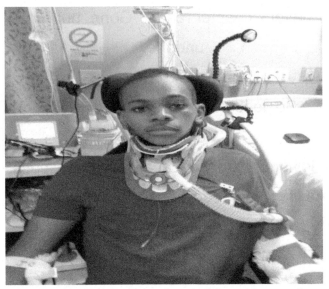

"Javar is growing stronger with each passing day. A testament to his unwavering determination and relentless commitment to personal Development."

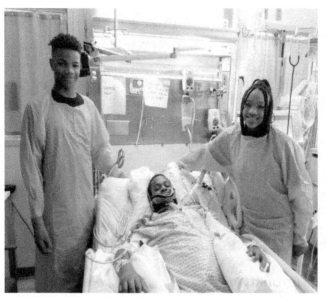

"One day at a time" Taking it one day at a time, Javar and his family move forward, embracing each moment with hope and determination."

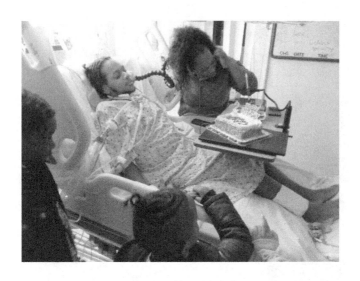

"Surrounded by family, Javar celebrates his 21st birthday, their smiles radiating joy and hope for brighter days ahead."

**Javar
12.03.21**

"Treasured memories, unseen yet deeply felt. In the tapestry of time, love's whispers echo, etching smiles on our hearts. Always in our thoughts, forever missed."

We Miss You Javar

" "Cherished moments live in our hearts." "

" "Treasured moments, an everlasting tribute." "

"Healing Connections: Resources for Finding Purpose Beyond Pain"

National Suicide Prevention Lifeline:

- Call: 1-800-273-TALK (1-800-273-8255)
- Available 24/7, confidential support for anyone in distress.

Grief Counseling Services (New Jersey):

RWJ Barnabas Health Grief Support Services:
- Website: https://www.rwjbh.org/griefsupport

Hackensack Meridian Health - Grief Support Services:
- Website: hackensackmeridianhealth.org/services/care-support/grief-support

New Jersey Hospice and Palliative Care Organization:
- Website: njhospice.org

Journey to Wellness - Grief Counseling Services:
- Website: journeytowellness.com

The Healing Center - New Jersey:
- Website: healingcenter.org/locations/new-jersey

Remember to check with these organizations directly to confirm their current services and availability. Additionally, local mental health providers or counseling centers may offer grief counseling services free or reduced.

Local Support Groups:
GriefShare Support Groups:
- Website: griefshare.org

Compassionate Friends - Central New Jersey Chapter:
- Website: compassionatefriends.org

RWJ Barnabas Health Grief Support Services:
- Website: rwjbh.org/griefsupport

Journey to Wellness - Grief Support Groups:
- Website: journeytowellness.com]

Always check with these organizations to confirm their current offerings and availability. Additionally, local churches, community centers, and counseling centers may also host grief support groups.

Online Grief Counseling:
BetterHelp
Website: www.betterhelp.com
Talkspace:
Website: talkspace.com
GriefShare Online:
Website: griefshare.org
Online-Therapy.com:
website: online-therapy.com
Regain:
Website: regain.us

Please research each platform to find the one that best suits your needs. Remember, reaching out is a sign of strength. You are not alone in this journey.

Made in the USA
Middletown, DE
07 June 2024